Joy Builder Devotional Workbook

Your Joy Blesses Others

W W W . J O Y C H A L L E N G E F O R M O M S . C O M

COPYRIGHT © 2017
TOMMY NEWBERRY . HELP CLUB FOR MOMS

Hello mamas, It's Deb from the Help Club for Moms!

Today we begin our journey to becoming more joyful moms—together. As with anything in life, we learn more when we have friends beside us to help us to learn, grow, and process what we are discovering. Not too long ago, our Help Club for Moms team journeyed with Tommy Newberry through The 40 Day Joy Challenge and applied what we learned to our marriages and our children. Having Tommy in our life felt like we had our own coach and helped us stay accountable to our goal of becoming joy-filled mamas.

We all remarked how our lives were changed and how we became more joyful in our everyday lives. We loved the challenge so much that we decided to share it with all of our mom friends.

The Joy Challenge for Moms is based on the unchanging word of God and is a useful tool to help you maintain lasting joy for years to come. To get the most out of the program, be sure to set aside time each day to watch the videos and complete the "Daily Joy Builder" worksheets.

If time is a factor, pray and ask God to get you up 15 minutes earlier each day to complete the challenge. In the orientation lesson (Day 0), I love how Tommy says, "I look forward to seeing you tomorrow, *bright and early!*" Getting up early and starting your day with God and The Joy Challenge for Moms is a fantastic way to become a more joyful mom. Who knows, you might even surprise yourself and decide you like being an early riser and continue this habit for many years to come.

GETTING STARTED

Here's how to get the most out of The Joy Challenge for Moms:

1. Pray! Make sure you pray and ask God to help you to get the most out of the videos and the Daily Joy Builder worksheets. Ask God to give you wisdom each day and to help you be the best Christian woman, wife, and mother you were created to be—today.

2. Print out the Daily Joy Builder worksheets and either staple them together or put them into a 3-ring binder so you don't lose them. Keep them near your Bible.

3. Pray with a prayer partner! A big component of the Help Club for Moms is praying for 10-15 minutes once a week with a friend. This one habit will truly change your life! Be sure to invite her to do The Joy Challenge for Moms with you. It's more fun to do things with a friend! If you don't know someone to pray with you, ask God to bring her to you. God is faithful and will provide!

4. Each Daily Joy Builder sheet contains a Mom Tip and a Joy-Filled Idea. Prayerfully complete each of these ideas. They will bless you and your family and help you to be a joyful, intentional mom.

5. Sign up to receive the text messages from Tommy, our Joy Coach. These texts are encouraging and inspiring and help you to stay focused!

6. Follow us on Facebook @HelpClubForMoms and join our online group @HelpClubForMoms Online Group and Instagram @HelpClubForMoms. Here you will be able to connect with other moms who are doing The Joy Challenge for Moms as well. We pray for each other and share inspiring posts and videos designed to help you to become the most joyful mom you can be!

We are so excited you are here with us! Remember, your joy blesses others!

DAY
0

"Orientation"

*"He settles the barren woman in her home,
as a joyful mother of children. Praise the Lord."*
- Psalm 113:9

Dearest mama, God wants you to find joy in your everyday life and be settled as a joyful mother. When we are joyful, our homes are fun and our kids feel secure. There is an old saying: "If mama ain't happy, ain't nobody happy." I have found this to be true in my life and the lives of the moms I know.

God wants to help us find true joy each day by relying on Him and focusing on the truth of the Scriptures. As you journey through The Joy Challenge for Moms, remember to ask Jesus to speak to your heart. He knows you, your kids, your husband, and your situation better than you do. He will help you each day. Make it your aim to spend this time with God and The Joy Challenge each day, and let God transform your life.

Blessings and love,
Deb

JOY-FILLED IDEA

- If you have upper-elementary kids or high-school-aged kids, consider doing The Joy Challenge for Moms together as a family! Everyone can benefit from having more joy in their lives! Watch the short videos together, and talk about the daily Scripture and the lesson.

- Make it even more fun by making a chart to track your progress as you complete each day's lessons. Don't worry if you miss a day; this is not a race. The main goal is that you finish, whether it's in 40 or 50 days, just make it fun and complete the challenge.

- When you finish the program, celebrate together as a family with a fun family activity!

THOUGHT OF THE DAY

YOUR  BLESSES OTHERS

MOM TIP

Purchase spiral-bound index cards on which you can write the Scriptures from each of the Daily Joy Builder Sheets. Keep them at your kitchen sink or somewhere you will see them each day.

Make it your aim to memorize the daily verses. Hiding God's Word in your heart will help you live a joy-filled life!

"I have told you this so that my joy may be in you and that your joy may be complete."
- John 15:11

"The Challenge & Promise of Joy"

Isn't is amazing to think that we were created for joy? The God of the universe values joy so much that He wants it to be a staple in our everyday lives, and He even gave us instructions in the Bible to help us accomplish it. When we read the whole chapter of John 15, we see Jesus providing the secret to life the way it was meant to be lived; we were meant to live life close to Jesus, obeying what His word says to us. One of the ways we obey is by giving our thoughts over to Christ.

I don't know about you, but I have trouble with my thoughts from time to time. I am really excited to begin The Joy Challenge for Moms and learn how to obey Jesus and think true thoughts in a way that pleases God and helps us become the Christian women, wives, and mothers we were created to be! After all, joy is contagious, and when we do what we need to do to keep our thoughts joyful, our whole family benefits from it! See you tomorrow!

Blessings and love,
Deb

JOY-FILLED IDEA

- Write a brief letter to God asking Him to help you to become all that He has created you to be in the power of the Holy Spirit. Tell Him some of the reasons why you want to have more joy in your life. Your reasons could be, "I want to have a better marriage and relationship with my kids," "I want my kids to have great memories of a joyful childhood," or "I want to cultivate a home filled with joy and laughter."

- Ask God for wisdom and help to learn and apply all you can from The Joy Challenge for Moms.

THOUGHT OF THE DAY

I WAS CREATED FOR *Joy*

MOM TIP

Have you found a prayer partner yet? If not, pray and ask God to bring you a fellow mom to pray with weekly.

Remember, this one habit will change your life and help you and your friend go deeper in your friendship.

"Finally, believers, whatever is true, whatever is honorable and worthy of respect, whatever is right and confirmed by God's word, whatever is pure and wholesome, whatever is lovely and brings peace, whatever is admirable and of good repute; if there is any excellence, if there is anything worthy of praise, think continually on these things [center your mind on them, and implant them in your heart]."
- Philippians 4:8 (AMP)

"The Challenge of Perspective"

THOUGHT
OF THE **DAY**

I SEE THE
Blessings
THAT SURROUND ME

MOM TIP

Tonight, before you go to bed, make sure you do the dishes and wipe out your sink. Waking up to a clean sink helps get your day off to a great start!

Hello, mama! Do you know someone in your life who always seems to be happy and joyful no matter what? I sure do! It looks as if nothing ever goes wrong for this person, right?! But in all actuality, we know this can't be true. Life deals out a fair share of good or bad cards to everyone, just as Tommy said in our lesson today. No one is exempt from bad stuff; it's continually sprinkled in with the good. The people in our lives who always appear joyful choose to see the blessings around them every day rather than the bad or negative. It gives them a good perspective. They have learned not to give unnecessary attention to evil.

This goes right along with what we learned in our lesson today: Joy is an automatic by-product when we think good thoughts. Think about it: We can be that person who lives a joyful lifestyle in our homes. We *can* fine-tune our perspective by controlling our thoughts about our kids or husband! Any person who uses self-control in her mind can be that person who radiates joy!

Blessings and love,
MariJo

JOY-FILLED IDEA

- Controlling our thoughts can be compared to controlling traffic on a busy street—we can be so busy in our minds that sometimes we forget to properly manage them. Ask God to help you be more aware of your thoughts and to help you focus on your blessings more than your problems.

- Make a list on paper: problem thoughts on one side & blessing thoughts on the other. Give your blessing thoughts a green light (let them flow), and give your problem thoughts a red one (cast down and replace them). If you don't know what to write or think on after you cast a negative thought down, just begin to pray and thank God for any blessing you can think of. Write down what you are thankful for instead. Shift your thoughts heavenward by replacing a negative mindset with a positive one. Mama, we create new, positive roads in our brain by doing that! Well-traveled roads of positive thought become highways over a short period of time. We can live a *life of joy* when we consistently meditate on good things!

"The thief only comes to steal and kill and destroy: I have come that they may have life and have it to the full."
- John 10:10

"The Challenge of Free Will"

Hello, dearest mama! Did you know that you have free will to choose your thoughts? To be honest, before I became a Christian and started learning about the Bible, I believed people couldn't help thinking negative thoughts. As a result, I lived in negativity for years complaining and feeling sorry for myself and my circumstances.

Satan tries to wage war in our minds, and he wants to steal our joy by making us believe lies about our lives. We will all have troubles and hard times in our lives, but if we choose to focus on the positive and not give power to the negative we will see a huge shift in the joy we feel.

So, how do we battle against Satan stealing our joy? We replace bad, negative thoughts with positive thoughts and truths from God's Word. When we choose to think about the blessings and good things in our lives more than the problems, we will automatically live lives characterized by joy. When we do this, we are living out 2 Corinthians 10:5, where it says to "cast down" the bad thoughts. Choose joy, mama, and don't give Satan power over your thoughts.

Blessings and love,
Brandi

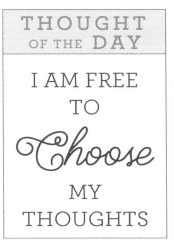

THOUGHT
OF THE DAY
I AM FREE
TO
Choose
MY
THOUGHTS

MOM TIP

A great way to build joy in your life is to plan your meals. This will alleviate stress and help you feel more organized.

Know what's for dinner by 9 a.m. each day this week.

JOY-FILLED IDEA

- A great way to be prepared for the battle in our minds is by keeping a list of positive truths on hand for the times when we start to feel the negative thoughts take over. Begin by dividing a piece of paper into two columns. In the left column, write a few of the negative thoughts you currently struggle with. In the right column, write positive and true thoughts to replace these negative thoughts. Be sure to include every small blessing and good thing you can think of that will counter the negative ones. Write a Scripture that helps you think true thoughts and combats the negative ones.

- The next time negative thoughts start to take over your thought life, you have your ammo of positive thoughts and Scriptures ready to replace these negative thoughts. Don't let Satan win the battle. Remember, we have free will to choose positive thoughts. You can do it, mama!

"'For I know the plans I have for you,' declares the Lord, 'plans to prosper you and not to harm you, plans to give you hope and a future.'"
- Jeremiah 29:11

"The Challenge of Trusting God"

Hey mama! Today, Tommy reminded us that we can choose joy! That sounds simple, but how do you choose joy? You choose joy by what you focus on! "He is a wise man (she is a wise mom) who does not grieve for the things which he has not but rejoices for those which he has." - Epictetus

The key is not to focus on what we *don't* have, but to rejoice about what we *do* have! This takes a conscious effort on our part because it's easier to see what's not working than to see what is working.

You cannot *think* two things at the same time. You cannot *feel* two things at the same time. Thinking on the bad makes you feel bad, while thinking on the good makes you feel good. Which one will you choose today? If you actively choose to think about your blessings, you are choosing joy and will start to feel that joy.

There is always something for which we can be joyful! Read the verse at the top of the page again: "God has a good future planned for you!" That alone is a reason for joy!

To miss out on joy is to miss out on the reason for your existence. – C.S. Lewis

Blessings and love,
Kathryn

JOY-FILLED IDEA

- Write a brief thank you note to God expressing appreciation for the good in your life and for the amazing future He has planned for you. Ask God to reveal the next most important steps you should take to bring about His will for your life.

MOM TIP

Find a container and make it your family's "Awesome Jar." Make it a habit to add one slip of paper to the jar each day celebrating the good things in our daily lives. If it was a bad day and you can't think of anything, then write, "We are all still alive today!"

The more good you notice today, the more you will notice tomorrow.

"You make known to me the path of life; in your presence there is fullness of joy; at your right hand are pleasures forevermore."
- Psalm 16:11

"The Challenge of His Presence"

Did you know it is possible to believe in Jesus without embracing the fullness of His presence and joy in your life? Tommy compares our potential lack of closeness with the Lord to a husband and wife who share a home but experience little attachment and intimacy. Just as marital intimacy requires effort and attention, walking daily in God's presence requires practice as well (Proverbs 3:5-6).

We can deepen our intimacy with the Savior by thanking Him continually throughout the day for all the small blessings He gives us (1 Thessalonians 5:16-18). We can release our mistakes to Him through repentance and saturate ourselves in Scripture, which is His love letter to us.

Soon, we will grow to find ourselves living a life of joy, spurred by His abundant grace (2 Peter 1:2)! We will hear His whispers of love, and our hearts will soften to His wisdom. My friend, God wants to refine you and minister to your mama-heart through His Word and His Spirit! Do not sacrifice that opportunity for the sake of being your own leader! Walk in the presence of Christ and allow Him to guide you on His path of joy!

Blessings and love,
Tara D.

> ### THOUGHT OF THE DAY
> GOD IS
> *Here*
> WITH ME
> RIGHT NOW

> ### MOM TIP
> Spend ten minutes reconnecting with your spouse today without any distractions. Turn off your cell phones and spend some time really talking with one another.

JOY-FILLED IDEA

- As Tommy suggested, a lack of intimacy in marriage can greatly deplete your joy! Take a moment to pray about how you can infuse more closeness into your marriage today.

- Begin by reflecting on your thoughts toward your husband. Each time you experience a negative thought about him, immediately replace it with a positive one. Remind yourself of the qualities you love about your husband and praise him for these attributes each day. Pray blessing and Scripture over your husband and endeavor to become his number one encourager!

- Memorize James 1:19-20: "Everyone should be quick to listen, slow to speak, and slow to anger, for man's [a wife's] anger does not bring about the righteousness that God desires." Apply it daily! When you are living in unity with your spouse, your heart will be open to the joy the Lord has for you.

JOY CHALLENGE *for Moms*

WITH **TOMMY NEWBERRY** & **HELP CLUB FOR MOMS**

"For you created my inmost being; you knit me together in my mother's womb. I praise you because I am fearfully and wonderfully made; your works are wonderful, I know that full well."
- Psalm 139: 13-14

"The Challenge of Identity Theft"

Hello, precious daughter of the King! Isn't it amazing to think about how much value you have? God created you as His beautiful daughter, and He has given *you* an identity like no one else's on Earth. However, due to life's circumstances, our self-worth can slowly begin to diminish. We start to believe the lie that we have no value, which robs us of our joy.

But you can say "no" to this mindset, mama! You are a strong, capable warrior! Remember that your true self-worth is only based on what God says about you and not on what other people say about you. God chose you for this time in your life. You have a beautiful purpose to be the wife and mother He created you to be. You are God's perfect choice for your children and husband!

As mothers, it is vitally important that we remain confident in our identity in Christ. We have little ones watching us, and if we stay focused on God's truth, our joy will overflow into how we speak and act. What a powerful way to demonstrate the truth of God and His purpose to your children!

Blessings and love,
Rachel

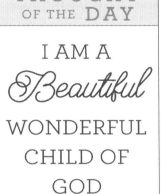

THOUGHT OF THE **DAY**

I AM A *Beautiful* WONDERFUL CHILD OF GOD

MOM TIP

Take 3 days this week and make a conscious choice to push all negative self-talk from your mind and mouth. Replace it with positive affirmations.

JOY-FILLED IDEA

• A practical way to be reminded of your true identity and how loved you are is to write a list of the wonderful qualities about yourself that you value and admire. These traits are unique to you and were given to you to magnify God's joy to others. Try to come up with at least five things about yourself that you love and then spend some time praying a prayer of thanksgiving to your Father for creating you with a purpose.

"...Whatever is true, whatever is noble, whatever is right,
whatever is pure, whatever is lovely, whatever is admirable—
if anything is excellent or praiseworthy—think about such things."
- Philippians 4:8

"The Challenge
of Focus"

You've probably heard the old adage, "You are what you eat." Your body is only as healthy as the quality of food you put into it! The same is true for your mind and heart, so you need to be very careful about what you fill yourself with mentally and physically. As Tommy wisely stated, "You will always feel what you focus on!"

For years, I believed that I wasn't a worthy mom because one of my sons would constantly misbehave. Over time, my feelings toward him turned to resentment and dislike, which made me feel even more condemned. These "feelings" were lies from the enemy that I was fueling by focusing on the negative attributes of my son and myself. When I realized this, I began to reject them as they came, calling out the God-given gifts in my son and myself instead. This shift has transformed our relationship, as well as his behavior, restoring my joy and confidence as a mother.

Romans 4:17 says, "God...calls into being things that were not." What does that mean for us as children of God? Focus on the truths of God's Word, rather than what you're feeling, and experience joy as never before!

Blessings and love,
Bek

THOUGHT OF THE DAY

MY FOCUS
Creates
MY FEELING

MOM TIP

Write Philippians 4:8 on a notecard and keep it in your car. Every time you get in your car to run an errand or pick up a child, read the verse aloud. Try to memorize the verse in a week.

JOY-FILLED IDEA

• What thoughts are you entertaining? Be honest with yourself and ask, "Am I dwelling on the negative attributes of myself, my children, or my husband?"
The mind is truly our greatest battlefield and the place where the enemy continually strikes. We must be watchful for these subtle attacks and rebuff them as they come by turning negative thoughts and emotions into proclamations of God's goodness and blessing! For instance, if a child is continually disobeying and causing frustration, instead of lamenting his faults, proclaim (in faith) that "he is an obedient, mighty man of God! I am so thankful for him!" These thoughts and declared blessings will begin to reshape your outlook, and your joy will be contagious for those around you!

"For I know the thoughts that I think toward you, says the Lord, thoughts of peace and not of evil, to give you a future and a hope."
- Jeremiah 29:11 (NKJV)

"The Challenge of Direction"

Hey, mama! Did you know that you were created with a purpose and destiny? God has goals for *all* of His children. He plants goals and assignments in our hearts so that we can live with determination. Perhaps you already know your calling and are actively working toward that objective, or maybe you haven't asked the Lord for clarity yet.

Goal-setting reveals what we want to see happen in our lives while allowing us to set tangible targets. It helps keep our focus off of our fears, flaws, doubts, and troubles, and it is also an essential tool to help you concentrate on what is lovely, excellent, and worthy.

Maybe your goal is to be a loving wife and mother—that is an excellent goal! God has a great calling on us as mothers! We are raising up the next generation of believers in Christ! It is a tremendous task that incites us daily to seek the Lord for wisdom. God's goal is not for us to be super-mommies but for us to be women who earnestly love Him and desire more of Him.

Blessings and love,
Rae-Ellen

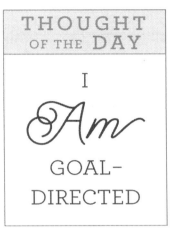

THOUGHT
OF THE DAY

I
Am
GOAL-
DIRECTED

MOM TIP

During your quiet time today, pray and ask the Lord about one goal He wants you to set in your life. Remember, make your goal S.M.A.R.T (specific, measurable, achievable, relevant and time-bound).

JOY-FILLED IDEA

• As moms, we tend to have goals not only for ourselves but also for our husbands and children. I am sure we all have good goals in mind, but we need to be careful to make sure they are lined up with God's will and not ours. Take some time to ask the Lord what His goals are; release your expectations, and receive God's grace today. Ask Him for new inspiration, and put them into writing as He reveals these new ambitions. Unwritten goals have no power in your life.

Habakkuk 2:2-3 (NKJV): "Write the vision and make it plain on tablets, that he may run who reads it. For the vision is yet for an appointed time; but at the end it will speak, and it will not lie. Though it tarries, wait for it; because it will surely come, it will not tarry."

*"Guard your heart above all else,
for it determines the course of your life."*
- *Proverbs 4:23*

"The Challenge of Productive Questions"

Throughout the process of building our house last year, I developed a habit. Like an inspector, I was on the lookout for things built incorrectly or needing to be fixed. Although necessary at first, it developed in me a habit of asking the wrong questions. One day, as I was driving away from the house with more bad news, God gently reminded me that Satan was successfully stealing my joy.

The trickiest part about life is maintaining our joy in the midst of disappointment.

After living in our new house for six months, God began to show me that my heart now needed a guard, not an inspector! I had to relearn how to ask myself joy-producing questions, such as, "What do I love about my house?"

The Bible is clear that guarding our hearts and focusing on God's Word will not only bring life and healing, but it will also determine our course!

Blessings and love,
Tara F.

THOUGHT OF THE DAY

WHAT ARE YOU *Thinking?*

MOM TIP

Spend extra time with your children today. If you can, spend one-on-one time with each of your children. Tell them five things you love and admire about them.

JOY-FILLED IDEA

• Ask God to help you choose one area of your life in which your questions need to change from fault-finding to faith-producing. For instance, as a mom, what are some things that you are doing *right*? How do you see God working in your child's life? What is your favorite thing about your child?

"This is the day that the Lord has made;
let us rejoice and be glad in it."
- Psalm 118:24 (ESV)

"The Challenge of Proactive Thinking"

Some people are able to rejoice and be glad no matter who or what has offended them. Do you know a mom who's like that? It's tempting to dismiss and criticize these friends as shallow.

Yet, let's unpeel the layers a bit. When someone hurts me, does it help to surrender my emotional control to that person? Did you know that no one can make you mad without your permission?

As provocative as these questions are, they are imperative to think about because the ones that hurt us the most are often the ones that love us the most: our husband and our children.

To be an effective, loving wife and mama, we need to keep our thoughts lined up with God's word. John 13:34 says, "Love one another. As I have loved you, so you must love one another." Also, the Bible reminds us that love is patient, kind, and not irritable or rude.

Before the difficult situation arises, we must plan ahead and consider our responses, so we can lovingly respond to our family every time. A proactive thinker can speak kindly and gently to her husband and children, even when things get tough!

Blessings and love,
Kristi

JOY-FILLED IDEA

- Our sweet families inadvertently press our buttons on a regular basis, so it's important to be prepared. In a quiet, peaceful moment, think of each typical scenario and make a list of them vertically down one side of a piece of paper. Next to each item, write down the ideal, kind, patient response that would bring glory to God and love to your family. Now you have your cheat sheet! Keep it with you and refer to it often when times get hard and your joy is challenged.

THOUGHT OF THE DAY

I'M A PROACTIVE *Thinker* AND IT SHOWS

MOM TIP

Start your morning by creating your "6 Most Important" list. What are the six most pressing issues on your schedule/to-do list? Write them down on your to-do list for the day, and concentrate on getting them accomplished first before adding new items to the list.

"But seek first his kingdom and his righteousness,
and all these things will be given to you as well."
- Matthew 6:33

"The Challenge of Early Mornings"

Today, Tommy challenges us to begin each day with God. As busy moms, it's easy to want to sleep until our children wake us up in the morning. However, waking to the demands of the day is no way to optimize our joy. To have a joy-filled day, we need to schedule our first minutes with our Heavenly Father. We have access to the all-knowing, all-powerful Creator of the universe!

Wake up at least 15 minutes earlier each day for your Early Morning Joy Ritual. What can you do in that time to prepare yourself mentally and spiritually?

1. Saturate your mind with Scripture.
2. Develop a prayer routine.
3. Review your personal mission statement, goals, and priorities.
4. Be still and remind yourself that God is in control.
5. Take time every day to re-surrender every area of your life to Him.
6. Contemplate the size and scope of God. Remind yourself that any problem is small compared to your Heavenly Father.

When we fill our hearts and minds with Scripture first thing in the morning and refocus our hearts on God's purpose for our lives, we are in the best position to love and guide our family with joy.

Blessings and love,
Jennifer

JOY-FILLED IDEA

• Get up *for* your children instead of *to* your children in the mornings. Set your alarm clock to wake up before your children—it's worth it!

THOUGHT OF THE **DAY**

I LAUNCH
EACH DAY
With
GOD

MOM TIP

Create a quiet time basket that has everything you need for your quiet time. Gather your Bible, journal, devotional, Bonus Joy Builders, music, and anything else that will help you create a joyful start to your day.

*"The prudent see danger and take refuge,
but the simple keep going and pay the penalty."*
- *Proverbs 27:12*

**"The Challenge
of Pausing"**

Self-examination is a powerful tool that can bring you joy by improving your life. It's tempting to go through our days on auto-pilot, repeating thoughts and habits that come naturally; however, pausing to examine your words, thoughts, and actions can help you make simple changes towards self-improvement.

It's important to pause and look critically at how you live your life, relate to your husband and friends, and raise your children. Determine the good as well as the bad. Increase your positive tendencies while taking effort to eliminate the negative. Even a small change makes a major impact when practiced intentionally and regularly.

Blessings and love,
Heather

THOUGHT
OF THE **DAY**

I'M
INTENTIONAL
ABOUT MY

JOY-FILLED IDEA

- At Help Club for Moms, we offer weekly Mom Tips in four important areas of motherhood: loving your husband, loving your children, caring for your home, and building your own spirit. At the end of the day today, consider how you did in each of these areas. Consider the good as well as the bad, and answer the following questions in your journal:

  1. What has been working?
  2. What has not been working?
  3. What do I need to improve/ do differently?

Make a habit of revisiting these questions on a regular basis—daily, weekly, monthly, or whatever works for you. Keep your answers in the same journal, so you have a log of your personal growth over time. You will be impressed with how much you can overcome when you consistently put forth the effort!

MOM TIP

Do the 5 o'clock pick-up right before your husband gets home from work. Set a timer for 15 minutes and have everyone help pick up the house. Pick up toys and other items that need to be returned to their proper home, put the mail away, wipe off the kitchen counters, etc. Continue to work until the timer dings.

"Fix your thoughts on what is true, and honorable, and right, and pure, and lovely, and admirable. Think about things that are excellent and worthy of praise."
- Philippians 4:8 (NLT)

"The Challenge of Marriage"

Today, we're going to examine the effect our thoughts have on our marriage. I'll never forget the first time I watched Dr. Brene Brown's video on the topic of blame. In it, she talks about dropping her coffee on the kitchen floor first thing in the morning and immediately blaming her husband. He had come home late the night before, so she declared the spill her husband's fault since she was tired from waiting up for him. For me, and millions of other viewers online, it was a hilariously relatable video.

Dr. Brown says her research has taught her that blame is a discharge of discomfort and pain. Blame has an inverse relationship with the vulnerable act of accountability. Instead of sharing how our feelings were hurt, we release anger. We miss an opportunity for empathy, connection, and joy. The thoughts we choose to entertain throughout our day significantly alter our marriages.

As a surf instructor, I would say, "Where your eyes go is where you will go." How do you want to be experiencing your spouse? Start thinking positively, and a positive experience will surely follow!

Blessings and love,
Brynne

THOUGHT OF THE DAY

I 4:8
MY
Mate!

MOM TIP

Take a moment today to pray for your spouse. Pray for his safety, his job, and your marriage. Ask the Lord to bring you closer together as a couple and closer to Himself.

JOY-FILLED IDEA

- If you have a negative thought about your husband, dig deeper to see if there is any piece of you that needs to be vulnerable with him regarding an unmet need or hurt feeling. Bravely choose the vulnerable route toward connection. Our marriage cannot afford the deadly debt of bitterness. Stay tender and use "I" instead of "you" statements that are more likely to be well-received. Then choose to become your husband's greatest cheerleader. Start with one positive affirmation of him in front of your kids. And finally, remember to take care of your own heart. Our joy will bless our husbands!

"May these words of my mouth and this meditation of my heart be pleasing in your sight, LORD, my Rock and my Redeemer."
- Psalm 19:14

"The Challenge of Shaking It Up"

All of us mamas fall into ruts. Some of these "ruts" may be good habits, like tucking our little ones in with a story each night, but other "ruts" may be robbing us—and those around us—of joy. Habits such as criticizing others, exasperation, and complaining cause those we love to shy away from us.

A friend of mine once told me, "Look at yourself in the mirror and make the face you would if you were scolding your kids. You look ugly!" I had never considered before how my children or spouse might see me as I criticized or condemned them. I tried her experiment, and she was right! I did look ugly—furrowed brows and mouth twisted into a scorn. This new knowledge revolutionized my thinking, and I chose to take a vacation from those "ugly ruts."

We all love the thought of vacation—leaving the normal routine and "shaking things up." So why not take a vacation from your negative thoughts and actions for a week as Tommy challenged? After all, what have you got to lose? Remember, you can always "return home" to the old way of doing things if you really miss it.

Blessings and love,
Bek

JOY-FILLED IDEA

- Take the time to write Philippians 4:8 and Psalm 19:14 on notecards and place them on your bathroom mirror, at your kitchen sink, and in your car. As you take your vacation this week from negativity, dwell on what is beautiful, excellent, true, just, and worthy of praise. Memorize these Scriptures by the end of the week!

- Treat yourself to some colorful flowers when you're at the grocery store this week and place them on your kitchen table. Each time you look at your bouquet of pure loveliness, be reminded of your "vacation" this week!

THOUGHT OF THE DAY

I AM
Rut Free
AND
REJUVENATED

MOM TIP

Compliment all the members of your family today. Smile at them and look them in the eye. While you compliment them, remember to tell them that you love them.

"Do not conform to the pattern of this world, but be transformed by the renewing of your mind. Then you will be able to test and approve what God's will is—his good, pleasing and perfect will."
- Romans 12:2

"The Challenge of Secret Conversations"

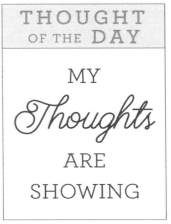

THOUGHT OF THE **DAY**

MY *Thoughts* ARE SHOWING

Dearest mama, do you ever take a moment to "think about what you're thinking about?" What are your thoughts towards your husband or the child who always gets on your nerves? If your relationship with your husband or one (or all) of your children is strained and hard, your thoughts may be the problem.

I love how Tommy says, "Your thoughts will eventually be revealed for everyone to see. A dream, a business, or a marriage dies first in the mind." This is so true! I have found that we tend to bring about what we think about. If you find your thoughts focused on your husband's or a child's shortcomings, that is what you will see the most.

My friend, God answers prayer! When you find yourself at odds with someone in your family, pray about it and then focus on the truth of God's Word. God hears every one of your prayers and will help you, your husband, and your kids love each other well. Jesus came so that we might have life abundantly, and part of abundant life is living in harmony with each other, especially within our families.

Blessings and love,
Deb

MOM TIP

Start your dishwasher before you go to bed. Let your dishwasher work while you sleep. Put away the clean dishes during breakfast time the next day.

JOY-FILLED IDEA

- Make it your aim to replace the negative thoughts with a true statement based on God's Word. The next time you find yourself thinking unproductive thoughts, say to yourself, "God hears my prayers and is helping me have a great marriage," or "God is helping me be a great mom!" Remember, God is with you and will help you love those in your life who are challenging to love. You are cooperating with God, and having loving relationships within your family is important to Him.

- Next, make the choice to speak words of life and faith. Call out the good in your husband and children. People will rise to what is expected of them!

"In everything give thanks: for this is the will of God in Christ Jesus concerning you."
- 1 Thessalonians 5:18 (KJV)

"The Challenge of Gratitude"

Today, Tommy's challenge intrigued me as he talked about how to be an exceptionally thankful person. I was so encouraged! I want to be remembered as an extravagantly grateful person, especially in my role as mom and wife. Since you're doing The Joy Challenge, you may feel the same.

In our world today, happy people sometimes get a bad rap; it's not normal or popular. Many people are negative, discouraged, and annoyed by joy. This reminds me of a cute book titled *Polly Anna*, a story about a little girl who played the *Glad Game*: a simple, fun exercise that helped people see their blessings. Her pleasant gratitude changed the attitude of the whole town to a positive mindset! Mom, we can turn the tide in our homes the same way she did, and live above the status quo. Exceptional thankfulness doesn't happen by chance. It happens by *choice*! It is a discipline that we can learn ourselves and teach our children.

When we focus on our blessings instead of our deficiencies, we are lifted into this emotional place of continual joy, a place in which we long to dwell. Let's become exceptionally grateful people, and make it normal.

Blessings and love,
MariJo

JOY-FILLED IDEA

- Let's put into practice what we learned about being grateful. Play the *Glad Game* while focusing on your future! Fast forward four years or more and meditate on the good changes that will take place over that period of time. Contemplate and imagine any future blessings that you will be experiencing at that point, and write up to eight of them in your journal or on your joy sheet. Then, go ahead: be glad in advance and thank God now, before any of it actually happens!

- Think of something good your husband has helped you with lately and send him a text of gratitude. Do it today!

THOUGHT OF THE DAY

I AM AN UNUSUALLY *Grateful* PERSON

MOM TIP

Take a moment during your quiet time to write thank you notes to three people, such as your children's teacher, your pastor, the mailman, your babysitter, or even the person who bags your groceries every week.

"I am the vine: you are the branches. If you remain in me and I in you, you will bear much fruit: apart from me you can do nothing."
- John 15:5

"The Challenge of Ingratitude"

Hey mama! Today, Tommy revealed to us how ingratitude can decrease the joy in our lives. Ingratitude is one of those sneaky things that makes its way into our lives. Gratefulness requires intentionality, but it comes much more easily when we take the time to connect with God daily. Just like John 15:5 says, when we are in Him, we bear much fruit. Gratitude is one of these fruits!

Sometimes, we busy moms feel ungrateful in our marriage. Whether we are just trying to survive or falling into the rut of a routine, we can forget to be grateful for everything our husbands do for us. Tommy refers to this as the *Law of Familiarity.* We can get so used to how our husbands bless us by doing things such as taking out the garbage, helping to put the kids to bed, cleaning up after dinner, or working hard to provide, that over time we forget to appreciate these things. We don't want this *Law of Familiarity* to keep us from appreciating our husbands, or worse, turn into feelings of entitlement or expectation. This will diminish not only our joy, but our husband's joy as well.

Blessings and love,
Brandi

JOY-FILLED IDEA

- This week, be intentional about seeing everything your husband truly does for your family. Pray and ask God to help you see him with new eyes. Everyday, tell him a characteristic about him or something that he does for you for which you are grateful.

- Try to be in the Word of God daily, even if it is just 5-10 minutes. We cannot have the fruit of the Spirit if we are not spending time in His Word.

- Take a moment to reflect on your life. Are there any other areas in which you may be harboring ingratitude and not even realizing it? Pray and ask God to open your own eyes to see areas of ingratitude and pray against them. Seek new things to appreciate.

THOUGHT OF THE **DAY**

I AM PREPARED FOR *Joy*

MOM TIP

Turn off your smartphone all day today. Focus on serving your family. Social media and your messages can wait until tomorrow. If this is truly challenging, allow yourself ten minutes at lunchtime to check messages on your phone.

"A man reaps what he sows."
- Galatians 6:7b

*"The Challenge
of the
Present Moment"*

Dear mama, today you have the *gift* of the present. There is no value in thinking negatively about the past or fearing something that might happen in the future. Enjoy this moment. Think about the good that's around you right now.

When you sow negative thoughts, you reap negative feelings. When you sow positive, faith-filled thoughts, you reap a positive attitude and joy! You have a choice.

When I find myself being negative, there are a couple of things I do to stop that train on its track. The first is to say a verse I have memorized. If I'm feeling overwhelmed—like I can't do it all, I say, "I can do all things through Christ." If I'm feeling fearful about something, I say out loud, "God has not given us a spirit of fear, but of love, power, and a sound mind." Another thing I do in a moment of anger or frustration is switch my thoughts to what I'm thankful for in that moment. This immediately takes the negative feelings away and replaces them with feelings of gratitude and joy. Joy is something we actively choose, moment by moment, thought by thought. Which will you choose today?

Blessings and love,
Kathryn

JOY-FILLED IDEA

- Wake up in the morning and say, "Today is the day that the Lord has made, I will REJOICE and be GLAD in it!" Say it with your kids throughout the day when you need to encourage them or yourself!

THOUGHT OF THE DAY

I
Cherish
THE PRESENT
MOMENT

MOM TIP

Choose one of the following Bible verses to teach your children:
- Galatians 6:7
- 2 Corinthians 9:6-7
- Philippians 4:6-7

"Your word is a lamp for my feet, a light on my path."
- Psalm 119:105

"The Challenge of What's True"

How many times have you been advised to "Follow your heart?" It's a popular philosophy in today's feelings-driven culture. However, real joy does not lie in doing what feels right. True joy is a product of submitting your feelings and emotions to the Lord and allowing Him to direct your decisions through the wisdom found in His infallible Word.

This applies so beautifully to our journey through motherhood and marriage! Are you feeling frustrated with your children? God tells us in Ephesians 4:2 to "bear with one another in love." You can do it, mama! When you are weak, He will be your strength (2 Corinthians 12:9-10). Are you anxious about a situation with your husband? Philippians 4:6 says to present your problems to God, and His peace will guard your heart as He works on your behalf.

As Tommy mentions, positive feelings are the reward after following the right path and putting your trust in the Lord (Isaiah 26:3). Do not let your feelings guide your life, my friend! Give them to the Lord, live in obedience to His Word, and expect real joy to follow!

Blessings and love,
Tara D.

THOUGHT OF THE DAY

I FILTER MY
Feelings
THROUGH GOD'S PROMISES

MOM TIP

When speaking to your spouse or children in a stressful situation, take an extra 30 seconds before responding. When we choose to respond in kindness, we are letting the light of Jesus shine through us.

JOY-FILLED IDEA

• As mothers, we teach our children to align their feelings with God's truths as well. Emotions are a gift from the Lord and can act as a barometer, warning us when something is amiss in our lives. However, we must not be mastered by those feelings! If our children are experiencing negative emotions, instead of simply giving in or silencing them, take the opportunity to help them learn to be proactive. Teach them to offer their negative feelings to the Lord and allow Him to redirect their hearts with His truth. Maybe your child is experiencing frustration over sharing a toy. Pray with him, discuss how God calls us to serve one another in love (Galatians 5:13), and help him think of a fun way to bless his sibling while he is waiting for a turn. Joy may not come immediately, but forming a habit of gently and kindly directing our children to the Lord will produce a great harvest of joy in their future!

"Therefore, prepare your minds for action; be self-controlled; set your hope fully on the grace to be given you when Jesus Christ is revealed."
- 1 Peter 1:13 *(NKJV - 1984)*

"The Challenge of RATS"

Hi, dearest mama! You made it to the halfway point in The Joy Challenge for Moms! I am so proud of you and am praying for you as you keep trekking along.

Today, Tommy warned us against the RATS in our lives, or, really negative thoughts. Negative thoughts can definitely feel powerful. They can be immobilizing and completely rob us of all joy. As mothers, it is crucial we dwell on the good stuff: things that are uplifting, working well in our lives, and worthy of praise.

The first step is to become aware of our negative emotions and thoughts and recognize we are being led by them. We must stop being the passenger and start being the driver. Often, our husband or our children do something that frustrates us, and we overreact or exaggerate. We rely too much on how we "feel" and stop looking at the facts. After all, feelings are never a substitute for the truth! These negative feelings and thoughts inevitably spiral out of control, and soon enough, our joy is gone.

But Christ overcame the world, which includes our thoughts—so hang on for an amazing ride as you continue to seek Him!

Blessings and love,
Rachel

JOY-FILLED IDEA

- Today was a hard lesson to hear. The good news is that you are only halfway, and Tommy still has so much wisdom to share about overcoming these RATS. The bad news is that the RATS might be very prevalent in your life. Let's take a close look at them right now. A powerful tool is to speak out loud the negative thoughts you are having, the ones that are currently in control of your emotions. Speak out against them! Jesus is stronger! Give these thoughts to Him and submit them completely at His feet.

THOUGHT OF THE **DAY**

MY
THINKING
Enriches
MY
EMOTIONS

MOM TIP

Start a load of laundry as soon as your day begins. Move it directly into the dryer. Fold it when it is dry and put it away immediately. Do not let the clean clothes sit around unfinished.

"Above all else, guard your heart,
for everything you do flows from it."
- Proverbs 4:23

"The Challenge
of Negative
Emotions"

When I think destructive thoughts, I know there is always a root cause. Feelings of discouragement, frustration, and negativity predictably occur if I am tired, hungry, or feeling disrespected or unloved. More often than not, it is a combination of a few of these unmet needs. When this happens, I have a choice. I can spew these life-sucking feelings onto those I love, or I can bottle them up. Either way, someone is going to feel the damaging effects, be it the recipient or me.

As Tommy stated today, "The more you think about something, the more it grows." What negative thoughts and feelings are you fueling each day by mentally running through them over and over? Charles Spurgeon said, "You cannot keep birds from flying over your head, but you can keep them from building a nest in your hair." Mama, we cannot help but feel the effects of negative thoughts or emotions from time to time, but we can help what we do with them!

Blessings and love,
Bek

THOUGHT OF THE DAY

GOD RULES
MY LIFE,
NOT MY

MOM TIP

Plan a fun dessert tonight for dinner. Pick a family favorite that you do not have very often. During dessert time, tell your family why they make you smile.

JOY-FILLED IDEA

- All throughout Proverbs, we find Scriptures stressing the importance of a healthy heart, the seat of your emotions. God desires us to manage our emotions well—not ignore them, and we need to trust in His wisdom! Write these verses down in a journal or on sticky notes where you will see them, and memorize a few of them over the next few weeks. If you want to take it one step further, discuss these verses with your children and work to memorize them as a family.

1. "A heart at peace gives life to the body, but envy rots the bones." Proverbs 14:30
2. "A happy heart makes the face cheerful, but heartache crushes the spirit." Proverbs 15:13
3. "The heart of the righteous weighs its answers, but the mouth of the wicked gushes evil." Proverbs 15:28
4. "A cheerful heart is good medicine, but a crushed spirit dries up the bones." Proverbs 17:22
5. "Listen, my son, and be wise, and set your heart on the right path..." Proverbs 23:19
6. "As water reflects the face, so one's life reflects the heart." Proverbs 27:19

"Whatever things are true, noble, just, pure, lovely, of good report, if there is anything of virtue and praiseworthy— meditate on these things."
- Philippians 4:8 (NKJV)

"The Challenge of Not Thinking Things"

You never have to have a receipt to exchange your thoughts.

I worked retail while in high school and college, so I know the ins and outs of returns and exchanges. If it doesn't fit right, look right, or if you find a better deal, you return it for your money back or exchange it for something else.

Today's culture exchanges everything, so shouldn't we exchange our thoughts that aren't right, too? It's called the *Law of Exchange*: returning junky thoughts for positive, fruitful, joy-producing thoughts. To nurture our thoughts, we need to be familiar with what the Bible says about what we should be pondering. Philippians 4:8 reminds us to think about things that are true, noble, just, pure, and lovely. Take a few minutes to meditate on this Scripture. Commit to memorizing it!

Blessings and love,
Rae-Ellen

THOUGHT
OF THE DAY

I'LL
JUST
Exchange
IT!

MOM TIP

Play praise and worship music in your home during the day (breakfast, lunch, quiet time, etc.) to help set the tone.

JOY-FILLED IDEA

- To keep negative thoughts from growing up as weeds in our minds, we need to align our thinking with God's Word. Tommy suggests taking inventory of our thoughts and becoming "hyper-sensitive" to our thinking patterns. If you are thinking a bad thought, be willing to upgrade it! This involves "switching the channel" when those impatient, self-loathing, envious, and offensive thoughts try to creep in.

- Another way to gauge "why we think/what we think" is by evaluating what you are filling yourself with. What are you watching? What are you listening to? Ask the Lord to show you if you have unhealthy influences or habits that are causing a mental war. Read and memorize the Word of God. It will equip you with God's truth and allow you to battle back by swapping fear for courage, doubt for faith, loneliness for hope, anger for love, worry for patience, and frustration with peace! Think on these things!

"Do not let any unwholesome talk come out of your mouths, but only what is helpful for building others up according to their needs, that it may benefit those who listen."
- Ephesians 4:29

"The Challenge of Nagging Thoughts"

Have you ever known anyone who has built their house on an active volcano? Of course not. Allowing negative thoughts to stick around is like living on the lava path and hoping an eruption doesn't occur. From my personal experience, it's just a matter of time.

Negative thoughts about ourselves and others are constantly coming into our mind—often spoken by Satan. It is our choice to let them take residence or send them packing. This is a difficult thing for many of us moms. God has designed us to be in touch with our emotions and with the desire to share these emotions with others.

I can attest that it feels much better to "vent" these thoughts and feelings to a friend. Even though it feels better temporarily, the Bible tells us that it is actually destructive. The tongue also is a fire, a world of evil among the parts of the body. It corrupts the whole body, sets the whole course of one's life on fire (James 3:6).

Not only can housing our negative thoughts harm us, they can hurt the friend we entrust with our burdens, and the person that has offended us. When a negative thought seeps into your mind, extinguish it right away before your joy is burned. Joy is fullest when we reside above our feelings.

Blessings and love,
Tara F.

JOY-FILLED IDEA

- Which negative thoughts are the usual problem causers you? Write down your thoughts and pick out some verses that will help you deal with these feelings in a productive way.

- Next time you are offended, write a journal entry to the Lord instead of picking up the phone. This is going to take building some serious self-control muscles. Are you in?

THOUGHT
OF THE DAY

I'LL
Defeat
NEGATIVITY

MOM TIP

Clear off any cluttered countertops or tables in your home today. Shred or throw away any unneccessary paperwork. Put away items that do not belong in certain areas. Commit to keeping the area you just cleared neat and tidy.

"We take every thought captive to obey Christ,"
- 2 Corinthians 10:5b

"The Challenge of Negative Emotions"

As I repeat the *Thought of the Day* in my head, I become more and more empowered. Say it again with me out loud, "I take responsibility for how I think!" Doesn't that feel good?

A thought comes in. I can choose to pay attention to it or let it pass by. Either I choose happy thoughts and reject negativity, or I flounder and let any old thought take root in me.

Colossians 3:2 says, "Set your mind on things above, not on earthly things." As a mom, you can devote yourself to digging deeper into God's design for parenting the sweet children He gave you instead of focusing on what your friends are doing. In your marriage, you can have a satisfying, godly partnership with your husband, turning your back on the world's standards and depressing statistics.

Have you ever thought about the consequences of not taking responsibility for your thought life? What you think about, you bring about! Did you know that most of us never think about controlling our thoughts and consequently, "wing it" through life? That can have devastating effects on our families. It's time to take responsibility for how we think!

Blessings and love,
Kristi

THOUGHT OF THE DAY

I AM RESPONSIBLE FOR HOW I *Think*

MOM TIP

Do a special activity with your children today. Pull out the paints or play-doh, or go for a nature walk. Talk about how we can see the beauty of God in all things and all people. Ask them to share examples with you while you create or explore.

JOY-FILLED IDEA

• Grab a dry-erase marker and write these three phrases on your bathroom mirror:
    1. "I take responsibility for how I think."
    2. "What I think about, I bring about."
    3. "I set my mind on things above."

Dry-erase markers work perfectly on mirrors and wash off completely. By the way, your children can join you in this effort. They will love the freedom of writing on the mirror! Every day, read the three sentences aloud and repeat them in your head throughout the day. If you're like me, old thought patterns are stubborn. It might take forty days, but slowly you'll notice your thought life move from negativity to joy!

*"As a father has compassion on his children,
so the Lord has compassion on those who fear Him."*
- Psalm 103:13

"The Challenge of Compassion"

As wives and mamas, we don't need to go far to meet a messy person who needs our compassion. As I watched today's video lesson, I couldn't help but think of the moody teenagers, obstinate toddlers, whiny preschoolers, fighting siblings, and grumpy husbands we face on a daily basis. We mamas have our work cut out for us! These blessings from Heaven, for whom we would give our lives, can be some of the most problematic people in our lives.

As we go through this Joy Challenge, we are learning to change our way of thinking, and now we are learning to change our way of reacting. As Tommy said, we must decide to react with compassion before the heat of the moment. To preserve our joy, we must decide not to take others' outbursts personally.

As I was writing this Joy Builder, my young son needed a haircut. I decided we should cut it shorter than ever. He was happy with the new haircut until dinner time, when he began to mourn the loss of his hair. I could have reacted defensively, but I decided not to take his emotional outburst personally and to respond with compassion. I reminded myself that his blood sugar was plummeting right before dinner. I did what I could to comfort him as a compassionate mom. Sure enough, after dinner, he announced he was all right with his haircut again. The episode had passed with my joy intact!

There is no easy way to become more compassionate. We become more compassionate as we walk through the fire and practice extending compassion to people who have been rude to us and have hurt us. Fluent compassion will come one decision at a time.

Blessings and love,
Jennifer

THOUGHT OF THE DAY

MY COMPASSION *Protects* MY JOY

MOM TIP

Write a note/make a treat for an elderly neighbor. If you do not have an elderly neighbor, adopt one from your church or a local nursing home. Remember to stay and visit for a little while. Elderly are often lonely and in need of fellowship, and they love visits!

JOY-FILLED IDEA

- Answer the question Tommy asked: "As a result of today's lesson, what is one way you will become more fluently compassionate?"

- Create a visual reminder to "clothe yourself with compassion" by writing Colossians 3:13 with dry-erase marker on your bathroom mirror, or post it on a notecard where you will see it each morning as you dress for the day.

*"Forget the former things; do not dwell on the past.
See, I am doing a new thing! I am making a way in the
wilderness and streams in the wasteland."*
- Isaiah 43:18-19

"The Challenge of Runaway Imaginations"

Why do we allow ourselves to dwell on past failures, fears, or seemingly hopeless circumstances and then apply them to the future? Do you see your child struggle in kindergarten and wonder how he will ever make it through 12 more years of school? After a small argument with your husband, do you jump to the conclusion that something is very wrong in your marriage? Admittedly, I have been guilty of this harmful mindset.

Friends, we are God's holy and dearly loved children, and our Father is capable of so much more than we could ever ask or imagine (Colossians 3:12, Ephesians 3:20). Therefore, we need to release our fears and anxiety to Jesus and trust that He is doing something new and beautiful in your life. He has a *good* future planned for you!

Blessings and love,
Heather

THOUGHT OF THE DAY

I
Envision
MORE
JOY

JOY-FILLED IDEA

- The issues that worry me most usually have the best outcomes because I commit them to God through prayer. Before you go to bed tonight, confess your mistakes, worries, and fears. Then ask God to cover over your sins, shortcomings, and fears. The purpose is not to pinpoint all your faults, but to give those areas to God through prayer. His strength is made perfect in our weakness (2 Corinthians 12:9). Allow yourself to imagine the good future he has planned for you, your children, and your marriage!

MOM TIP

Find a verse to quote when your imagination is running in a negative direction. If you are fearful that something bad is going to happen to your children, speak I Chronicles 17:11 over them: "When your days are over and you go to be with your ancestors, I **will** raise up your offspring to **succeed** you, one of your own **sons**, and I **will** establish his kingdom."

J☺Y CHALLENGE *for Moms*

WITH **TOMMY NEWBERRY** & **HELP CLUB FOR MOMS**

"A good person produces good things from the treasury of a good heart...What you say flows from what is in your heart."
- Luke 6:45 (NLT)

"The Challenge of Environment"

Hey, mama! Today, we are talking about preserving joy by protecting our hearts and minds from the hazardous influences of life.

When I first became a mom, I realized that no matter which "type" of mom I was going to decide to be, there would always be an oppositional "camp" of motherhood thinking. Whether I breastfed or bottle-fed, home-made organic baby food or bought it, co-slept or crib-slept my baby, not everyone would ever completely agree with how I mothered. I desperately wanted to be viewed as the best mom I could be for my kids.

When I took my eyes off Jesus to focus on what other moms were doing for their children, comparison hindered my strengths as a mother.

As long as we intentionally meditate on God's Word and reflect the person of Jesus concerning every family decision, we should be confident in our choices. As mother and author Leanna Tankersly says, "The one thing we can control is how we treat ourselves, and that one thing can change everything."

Blessings and love,
Brynne

THOUGHT OF THE DAY

I AM A *Sponge!*

MOM TIP

Write Proverbs 4:23 in your journal and on a notecard to place above your kitchen sink. Read it while you are doing your dishes. Try to memorize it in a week. Teach it to your children when they are sitting at the table for mealtime.

JOY-FILLED IDEA

- A practical way to improve the surroundings that affect your self-perceptions as a mother is to pay attention to the people you follow on social media. Make it easier for you to feel confident in the Spirit-led choices you're making for your family. Tell your accountability partner about any area of insecurity so that they can speak God's loving truth over you. God has great joy for us right behind the pain of our self-doubt!

*"I press on toward the goal to win the prize for which
God has called me heavenward in Christ Jesus."*
- Philippians 3:14

"The Challenge of Impulsivity"

What is an impulse? Webster's Dictionary defines *impulse* as being "the influence of a particular feeling," or a "sudden, involuntary inclination prompting to action." Either way, it is apparent that impulsivity is based on current feelings rather than deliberate planning.

As a mother of four, I have made numerous mistakes, and I have had to humbly repent and seek the forgiveness of my children. The majority of these blunders were due to following the negative *impulse* of the moment, rather than choosing to deal with frustration in a Christ-like way. Mama, just as Tommy stated, negative emotions are *not* God's will for your life (John 10:10). You were made for joy!

Do you *really* want joy? Your loving Healer is asking, *"Do you want to get well?"* (John 5:6). If the answer is yes, then what is your goal? If we do not have an objective, we will continue to give in to impulsivity because we are not living with the end in mind. Just as a competitor plans her route to the finish line, we need to plan our route for living as godly wives and mothers!

Blessings and love,
Bek

THOUGHT OF THE DAY

WHAT'S THE *Goal* HERE?

MOM TIP

Find a reason/way to say yes (within reason) to your children's requests today instead of immediately saying no. Be creative and kind. Remember, they are still small and we only have them in our homes for a short time.

JOY-FILLED IDEA

- Write Psalm 90:12 on a notecard and place it on your bathroom mirror. Memorize this verse: "Teach us to number our days, that we may gain a heart of wisdom."

- Write down a list of your *main* goals as a mother. Ask yourself these questions:

  1. When my children leave my care, what legacy would I like them to carry for the rest of their lives?

  2. What sort of relationship do I desire to have with my children? What sort of relationship do I desire my children to have with each other?

  3. How do I want my children to see themselves? How do I want them to see me?

"Consider it pure joy, my brothers and sisters, whenever you face trials of many kinds, because you know that the testing of your faith produces perseverance. Let perseverance finish its work so that you may be mature and complete, not lacking anything."
– James 1: 2-4

"The Challenge of Adversity"

Hello, friend. I don't know about you, but today's lesson really hit home for me. Oh, how I wish I could look at adversity as a friend and a tool for my growth, but the truth is, when I am going through a difficult season, I just want it to end as quickly as possible. I want nothing to do with trouble and difficulty! During trials, I often get angry, fearful, or even resentful. Adversity has a way of showing us what's inside of us, whether it's good or bad, holy or unrighteous. If you're like me, you want desperately to respond with grace and love, patience and kindness but constantly fall short.

This is where the power of Jesus comes in! Jesus doesn't want you or me to do anything apart from Him, much less deal with trials. Instead, He wants us to hold His hand and walk through the trials with Him, letting Him lead the way. Jesus is the One who will help you respond in a godly manner to difficulties, or if you fail, He will help you get back up again.

Blessings and love,
Deb

THOUGHT OF THE DAY

I GET
BACK
UP
Again

MOM TIP

Write James 1:4-8 on your chalkboard or bathroom mirror (in dry-erase marker). Read it every time you go in and out of the room in which the verse is written. Memorize the Scripture.

JOY-FILLED IDEA

• The best way to develop godly character is to have a daily time with Jesus. Consider setting aside 30 minutes a day for Bible reading and journaling, preferably at the beginning of the day. This one change in your life will make you more like Jesus than anything else. Try this for the next 30 days. Reward yourself with a prize when you've finished.

"Do not let any unwholesome talk come out of your mouths, but only what is helpful for building others up according to their needs, that it may benefit those who listen."
- Ephesians 4:29

"The Challenge of Destructive Words"

Today, we learned how incredibly powerful our words are. They can either encourage or discourage, motivate or deflate, generate joy or repel it. Like a steering wheel on a car, they control which way we go! They lead us to experience *life* or *destruction.* Speaking truth is good; speaking lies is bad. Do our words draw people *to* God or *away* from Him? Do our prayers and everyday speech agree?

If you find yourself muttering negative or destructive self-talk, today can be the day you choose to change that! As Tommy said, the words you speak today influence your world tomorrow. If you want to see life in everything you do, you need to give life to your thoughts, which in turn gives life to your words. Our words influence our thoughts and vice versa. God has given us power to prosper both ways! We believe what we speak, and we speak what we believe. The key to joy comes when we believe the right things (the things God speaks), and then use our tongue to agree with Him. In this way, we can prophesy good things into our present and future!

Blessings and love,
MariJo

THOUGHT OF THE DAY

I SPEAK

Life,
AND
I SPREAD

Joy

JOY-FILLED IDEA

- Think about it: It's one thing for other people to fill us with junk, but it's even worse when we choose to feed ourselves with toxic thoughts when we have our own free will! Has this become a habit in your life? Identify a few limiting things you've said to yourself or your family lately. In your journal, write the positive opposite of these negative thoughts and mutterings. Pray and ask God to give you a verse that points you to the actual truth of His Word instead. Believe what He says!

MOM TIP

Meal-plan for the week today. Decide what your family will have for dinner and create a grocery list. Hang your meal plan on your refrigerator and put your grocery list in your car. This way you will not leave your list at home when you venture out to the grocery store.

"By your words you will be justified,
and by your words you will be condemned."
- Matthew 12:37 (ESV)

"The Challenge
of Telling
the Truth"

What a great lesson today! Personally, I always perceive affirmation to be a positive thing, but Tommy showed us we can be affirming negative things in our life as well! Mind blown. It's totally true. If we choose to affirm negative things in our life, such as health issues, marriage problems, struggles with a difficult child, or even statements like, "Ugh, today is going to be an awful day," then we are choosing to claim these negatives in our lives. Friends, we don't have to!

Matthew 12:37 says, "By your words you will be justified, and by your words you will be condemned." Words can bring death, sweet mama, or they can bring life. Now that we know the power of affirmation, let's choose to only affirm the blessings in our lives and disclaim the negatives.

Ephesians 3:20 says that God can do more than we ask or imagine. Mama, instead of trying to do this all on our own, let's seek God and ask Him to show us our blessings and transform our thinking. Affirming God's goodness helps us declare the blessings He's placed in our lives.

Blessings and love,
Brandi

JOY-FILLED IDEA

- *Hey mama,* a great way to affirm the blessings in your life is to keep a gratitude journal. Get a small journal or notebook in which you can keep track of your blessings. Write a minimum of five things that you are thankful for each day. Look to even the smallest things around you that bring you joy. Some days might be harder than others, but keep at it. On those difficult days, look back through your journal and see all the blessings that God has placed in your life.

THOUGHT
OF THE **DAY**

THE WORDS
I USE

Shape
THE WORLD
I SEE

MOM TIP

Write this quote by King Solomon somewhere you can see it: "Words kill, words give life; they're either poison or fruit—you choose."

Plant seeds with your children and talk about the importance of speaking to each other with kindness. Place your potted seeds on your kitchen table as a visible reminder for everyone.

THE 40 DAY
J☺Y CHALLENGE *for Moms*
WITH **TOMMY NEWBERRY** & **HELP CLUB FOR MOMS**

*"Seek first his kingdom and his righteousness,
and all these things will be given to you as well."*
- Matthew 6:33

*"The Challenge
of Envy"*

Hello, mama! Do you know that God wants you to succeed as a mother? He will help you reach your potential if you seek Him. When you do your best at raising your children, you are making your home and this world a better place. When you see other mamas who are doing a great job and "succeeding," are you genuinely happy for them, or do you feel envious? Refuse to allow envy to poison your joy. Instead, thank God for their success.

Just as you cheer your children on, God wants you to cheer other moms on as well. God's success system allows for each of us to shine brightly! Talking about the negatives in others brings out the negative in you. However, recognizing and calling out the good you see in other mamas allows the good to grow in you! Support and encourage other moms towards success and allow other moms to support you.

I pray that you will have a joy-filled day!

Blessings and love,
Kathryn

JOY-FILLED IDEA

- Pray for those moms you see doing well, and ask God to instill traits in you that you admire in them. Ask God to bless them! Ask God to free you from all envy and jealousy and to make you genuinely happy when you see others doing well.

THOUGHT OF THE DAY

WHEN
OTHER
PEOPLE

Succeed,
IT BRINGS
ME JOY

MOM TIP

Make your bed as soon as you get up in the morning. It is a great start to the day, and your bedroom will look clean and uncluttered.

*"These things I have spoken to you, that my joy may be in you,
and that your joy may be full."*
- John 15:11 (ESV)

**"The Challenge of
Mission or Mood"**

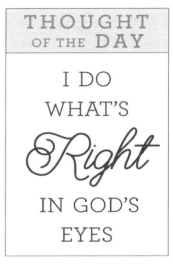

THOUGHT
OF THE **DAY**

I DO
WHAT'S
Right
IN GOD'S
EYES

Motherhood is so exhausting at times, isn't it? Under your care are little people with so many needs. Moreover, you carry the responsibility of discipling your children in Christ. Do you ever wake up wondering if you have lost your joy somewhere along the way? I do too, sister. However, the beauty of our relationship with Christ is that God's truth stands firm, regardless of our feelings (Psalm 119:89). Our joy is never truly lost because this joy is a gift from God. We can access it by plugging into His Word and walking in relationship with Him.

As Tommy says, we must practice intention over indulgence and must adopt a positive life mission that surpasses our unsteady moods. If you want to experience joy, commit to practicing that joy even when positive feelings do not come naturally. Take captive every negative thought and replace it with God's truth (2 Corinthians 10:5). Choosing to follow the Lord daily will bring peace, even in the midst of the chaos and exhaustion of motherhood. When you behave in a way that is consistent with Scripture, you will experience the joy that comes from pleasing your Creator, Savior, and Lover of your soul.

Blessings and love,
Tara D.

JOY-FILLED IDEA

- Choose to practice joy in the midst of busyness by noticing small blessings around you or reflecting on a verse from God's Word. Bring joy to your children and husband by assuming the best about them and replacing negative thoughts toward them with positive ones.

- Identify your mission as a mother. When you picture a joy-filled mother, what attributes come to mind? Make a list of those qualities and begin practicing them, even if they are not what comes naturally to you. Joy is a daily choice and a habit that must be honed. Determine who you want to be and practice becoming that woman today!

MOM TIP

Spend time during your quiet time praying and specifically asking God to give your life direction and purpose. Ask Him to reveal His plans for you in a mighty way.

"Many are the plans in a person's heart,
but it is the Lord's purpose that prevails."
- Proverbs 19:21

"The Challenge of Being on Purpose"

Hi, mama! Life sure is full of twists and turns, isn't it? Every decision we make can potentially affect another decision, and it is hard to know what God's purpose is for our life. Although it's hard, we need to come to the Lord through prayer and courage and humbly seek His will for our lives.

Before I really understood this, I often chose the easier path of conformity rather than discerning what was best for me—that is, the gifts and talents God uniquely instilled into me. Ultimately, I made some sacrifices and began to work for Young Life, and it was one of the best seasons of my life! I felt unbelievable joy, and I was a happier wife and mother. I knew I was truly living out my purpose.

I would like to challenge you not to conform to an ordinary life. You were created to be an outstanding mama, not an average one! Be original and have confidence in knowing that God only made one you. You were created for joy and for maintaining joy through your life. Modeling that joy to your children is one of the best gifts you can give them!

Blessings and love,
Rachel

JOY-FILLED IDEA

- Pray about your purpose. If you are confident that you are living in the will of the Lord for your life, then up the ante! How can you show even more joy to your kids? How can you help your children discover their gifts, talents, and purposes? If they are under 10, simply chat with them about what they like to do. Brainstorm unique things about each one of your children, and make a beautiful collage with the words and images. This will bless their hearts!

THOUGHT OF THE DAY

WELL DONE, MY GOOD AND FAITHFUL *Servant!*

MOM TIP

Declare a No-TV day in your home. If you are so moved, make it a week. Encourage reading, drawing, listening to music, or playing board games.

*"Whatever you do, work at it with all your heart,
as working for the Lord..."*
- Colossians 3:23

"The Challenge of Excellence"

If you're like me, there are days when you're tempted to throw in your "mommy towel" because you feel exhausted, frustrated, and discouraged. After all, motherhood is hard work! But, as Tommy said, our work is part of God's plan for us. And thank goodness, since it requires a significant part of our lives on Earth! When you serve your family with excellence, you will experience rich, lasting joy!

Mama, the Word of God, which is infallible, says that our work is a gift from God—not a punishment. God uses our triumphs and our struggles as mothers to grow us spiritually. For example, I have a child who seems to continually push the boundaries in every area, and I have felt like a failure on more than one occasion because of the behavior that comes from him. I struggle. I also pray. I pray for this child's heart, and I proclaim the promises of God over this young man. God has used this work to mature me and challenge me in ways I wouldn't otherwise be challenged. Your part, dear mama, is to stay in the fight so you can lay hold of the joy that comes with victory!

Blessings and love,
Bek

THOUGHT OF THE DAY

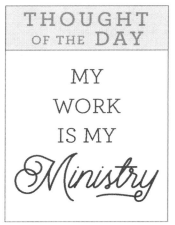

MY WORK IS MY *Ministry*

MOM TIP

When you wake up in the morning, before you get out of bed, commit your day to God. Ask Him to bless all those you are going to come in contact with that day and allow your schedule to flow freely. At the end of the day, remember to thank Him for the day that He provided you.

JOY-FILLED IDEA

- Hiding God's Word in your heart is like storing water in your hump if you were a camel, so when you're in the "desert" experiencing challenges of finding joy in your ministry as mothers, wives, and women of God, you can pull from your reserves and refresh your spirit! Write these Scriptures down in a journal or on notecards, repeating them until you've memorized each one.

  1. Genesis 2:15 - "The Lord God took the man and put him in the Garden of Eden to work it and take care of it."

  2. Ecclesiastes 9:10 - "Whatever your hand finds to do, do it with all your might..."

  3. 1 Corinthians 10:31 - "So whether you eat or drink or whatever you do, do it all for the glory of God."

  4. Proverbs 22:29 - "Do you see someone skilled in their work? They will serve before kings; they will not serve before officials of low rank."

"Rejoice in the Lord always. Again I will say, rejoice!"
- Philippians 4:4

"The Challenge of Taking Every Thought Captive"

Have you ever met another mom who was so full of joy that she radiated Jesus? I have had the pleasure of knowing such a woman, and of course, I wanted a slice of whatever she was having! Her joy was contagious! As Christians, we should be shining like a light on a hill (Matthew 5:14-15), so that people feel compelled to ask us what makes us different from the rest of the world! In today's lesson, Tommy shares that living a life of joy should be our goal and that our actions will speak louder than our words. He mentions that it is our *responsibility* to demonstrate joy and draw others to the Kingdom of God! It is our privilege to show the presence of the Lord in our lives and to make our joy known!

Are you living with this kind of joy? You might say, "Well, if my circumstances were different, if I didn't have a crying baby who kept me up all night, or if I didn't have a difficult child, then I would smile more...I would be more cheerful." Tommy says that joy needs to be developed. The Bible tells us to rejoice *always*! Exemplifying joy, despite our current situation, is an evident sign of spiritual maturity. Is there anything about our faith that glorifies God more than our joy? It is God's intention for all of His children to be joy-filled and to radiate His love!

Blessings and love,
Rae-Ellen

THOUGHT OF THE DAY

MY *Joy* IS CONTAGIOUS

MOM TIP

Say, "Good Morning" and "Hello" to all of your family members every time they enter the room. We often overlook those that are closest to us. Remember to smile when you see your loved ones!

JOY-FILLED IDEA

• Ask God to remind you of a time when you might not have reflected His joy with your actions. Confess your sin and ask your Heavenly Father to fill you with abundant joy so that it overflows into your actions and words. What looks irresistible to the rest of the world? Joy!

"Just as our bodies have many parts and each part has a special function, so it is with Christ's body. We are many parts of one body, and we all belong to each other."
- Romans 12:4-5 *(NLT)*

"The Challenge of Fixing Weaknesses"

When God made you, He was perfectly intentional. He planted in you the very seed and purpose of Heaven. He gave you the exact talents, personality, and intelligence, to function efficiently within the body of Christ; to fulfill His ultimate plan.

I have gone through most of my life believing that I had no talents. I look around and see the obvious gifting of others and feel inferior. I could give you a long list of things that I wish I was good at, or I could tell you the few things I can do for God's Kingdom. Howard Gardner did humankind a favor when he developed his theory of multiple intelligences. He noted that you cannot rightly assess a person based on IQ, but must take their whole potential into account.

These intelligences are:
- Spatial intelligence (creative, visual, artistic, remembers faces or scenes)
- Bodily-Kinesthetic intelligence (sports, drama, dance, building)
- Musical intelligence (musical and rhythmic)
- Naturalist intelligence (connect to and understand nature, love for animals)
- Linguistic intelligence (writing, reading, talking, debating)
- Logical-mathematical intelligence (works well with numbers, experiments, problem solves)
- Interpersonal intelligence (leader, conflict solver, communicator, makes friends easily, relates well to others)
- Intrapersonal intelligence (recognizes strengths and weaknesses, independent, goal setter, self-aware)

Understanding your God given ability and preferences will maximize your joy and the joy of others with whom you interact.

Blessings and love,
Tara F.

JOY-FILLED IDEA

- How about you, what are your intelligences? How is God calling you to use them for His Glory right now and in the future?

THOUGHT OF THE DAY

I
Focus
ON MY
STRENGTHS

MOM TIP

Pray with your spouse before he leaves for work and with your children before you go about your day. Ask God to bless their day and keep them safe.

JOY CHALLENGE *for Moms*

"I can do all things through Christ who gives me strength."
- Philippians 4:13 (BSB)

"The Challenge of Mental Discipline"

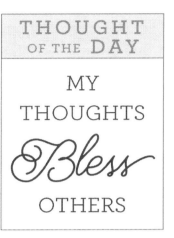

THOUGHT OF THE DAY

MY THOUGHTS *Bless* OTHERS

We think. We feel. We act. We become.

Because our thoughts accumulate and affect who we are in every area of our lives, we have to stay centered on productive thoughts!

In the same way an athlete develops strong muscles, we can train our mental "muscles" to be toned and effective, so that we can accomplish the plan God has for our lives. Mental laziness slowly dissolves our God-given potential.

How can you keep your thought life in top shape in order to bless your family? First, ask God to show you His divine calling on your life. 2 Peter 1:10 says, "Be all the more diligent to confirm your calling, for if you practice these qualities you will never fall." Jeremiah 33:3 says, "Call to me and I will answer you, and will tell you great and hidden things that you have not known."

Then, as God speaks to you, write down the goals He sets for you as mama of your family. Finally, walk confidently in the direction He gives you, believing that He will do immeasurably more than you can imagine.

Diligently focusing your thoughts on God's plan for you and your family will bless them immensely!

Blessings and love,
Kristi

MOM TIP

Turn off your smartphone after dinner. Choose to read a self-improvement book, listen to a podcast, or work on a project that you have been neglecting after your children have gone to bed.

JOY-FILLED IDEA

- Every mama needs a game plan. Hitting small goals, one at a time, means hitting the large goals in the end. You have eighteen years to raise your child, but it happens one day at a time. Prayerfully take the time to set strong, specific goals for your family, both for the long-term and the short-term. For example, our family has a vision statement that declares who we are in Christ and our values, based on the Bible. We also have yearly goals regarding growth in Christ, relationships, health, and finances, which line up with our family vision statement. And finally, each day, we distribute our goals into daily tasks. Yes, it takes discipline to walk through this exercise. But it is priceless to lay down in bed at night, knowing that you have earnestly put into practice God's divine direction for your family.

"For God is not a God of disorder but of peace."
- 1 Corinthians 14:33

"The Challenge of Clutter"

Sweet friend, we all become burdened by clutter at times. I'm not just talking about the kind of clutter that accumulates in closets and on countertops—I'm talking about mental, emotional, and spiritual clutter too. A messy closet or countertop gets in the way of everything you're trying to do in that space, so if you want to use your home for its intended purpose, you must clear the clutter away first.

Your mind and your spirit work in the same way, so if you want to maximize your joy, first you must minimize the clutter. It's that simple! Focus on disposing of negative emotions and thoughts in order to make room in your mind and in your heart for that which is lovely, pure, true, and excellent.

Blessings and love,
Heather

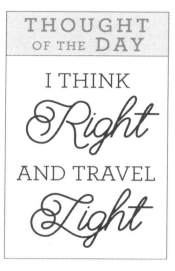

THOUGHT OF THE **DAY**

I THINK *Right* AND TRAVEL *Light*

JOY-FILLED IDEA

- Let's take action today by de-cluttering the most pressing areas of our lives!

  - Are you overburdened or overscheduled? Take ten minutes to examine your calendar, see what you can remove, and schedule time to focus on what God is teaching you.

  - Are your relationships suffering as you cling to hurt or bitterness? Set aside those ten minutes to pray about what is on your heart and then take a step to heal that relationship. If you've been at odds with your husband or one of your children, set aside one-on-one time to get some ice cream or coffee and nurture that relationship.

  - Maybe it's physical clutter that weighs you down. Then grab some trash bags, crank up the worship songs, and tackle that clutter until it is gone! Whether it takes one long weekend or several weeks of daily 15-minute spurts, keep at it until you finish the job.

MOM TIP

Clean out a closet in your home today. Take items that are no longer wanted to Goodwill right away. Commit to keeping the closet neat and tidy.

"May the God of hope fill you with all joy and peace as you trust in him, so that you may overflow with hope by the power of the Holy Spirit."
- Romans 15:13

You did it! The Joy Challenge is officially over, and now it is time to live out what Tommy has been teaching you. Joy is available to you today, but let's talk for a moment about the things that may hinder this new joy in the next few weeks. Remember the two most amazing promises from the Lord:

1. You are forgiven.
2. Heaven is near!

Remember that we feel what we dwell on, and we soak up our surroundings.

I want to encourage you to create a peaceful atmosphere in your home. This peaceful atmosphere will elevate your joy and rub off on your husband and children. As mothers, we are given the honor of cultivating our homes into calm and joyful places. Your joy starts at home and moves into the workplace, church, and everyday conversations with friends. Focus on lifting up these relationships and dwelling on your blessings. Joy will follow!

We are so proud of you!

Blessings and love,
Rachel

JOY-FILLED IDEA

- What are the most impactful things you have learned from this challenge— the lessons from Tommy that you never want to forget? Write them down in your journal and take time to hide them away in your heart. Write a few words on some note cards and place them around the house.

THOUGHT OF THE DAY

MY *Joy* BLESSES OTHERS

MOM TIP

I encourage you to talk to someone close to you about The Joy Challenge. Share what you've learned, and be honest about the lessons you need to apply to your life.

Ask that person to help keep you accountable by checking in with you in a week, and again in a month. Have them ask what you've been doing differently since completing The Joy Challenge. Keep positive changes in the forefront of your mind!

Tommy Newberry is a *Wall Street Journal* and *New York Times* best-selling author. He is the founder of The 1% Club and head coach of Tommy Newberry Coaching. These organizations are dedicated to helping entrepreneurs and their families maximize their God-given potential. Since 1991, Tommy has equipped business leaders in more than thirty industries to work less, earn more, and create greater significance with the right accomplishments.

He is the author of seven books, including the #3 New York Times bestseller, *The 4:8 Principle*, and the motivational classic, *Success is Not an Accident* both of which have been translated into a dozen languages.

In 1999, Tommy created the acclaimed Couples Planning Retreat which took world-class planning tools into the family realm, allowing husbands and wives to design a more balanced, simplified, and enriching life together.

Tommy is frequently invited to speak at schools, parent support groups, churches, and business conferences. He's appeared as a guest on over 200 radio and television programs, including Good News, Living the Life, Fox & Friends, The Lou Dobbs Show, Your World With Neil Cavuto, Janet Parshall's America, The Fox News Strategy Room, Everyday with Lisa & Marcus and many others.

You can connect with Tommy at TommyNewberry.com, on Facebook @TommyNewberry and @The40DayJoyChallenge, and on Instagram @CoachTommyNewberry.

Tommy lives in Atlanta, Georgia with his wife, Kristin, and their three boys.

Help Club For Moms is a group of real moms who seek to grow closer to God, closer to our families, and closer to each other. We believe prayer changes everything and God is big enough to help us raise the children with whom God has blessed us.

We focus on digging into God's Word, praying together, and encouraging one another! Through weekly "Mom Tips" and daily "Faith Filled Ideas," the Help Club for Moms helps women take what they are learning about the Lord and apply it to their daily journey as wives and mothers. Our goal is to spread the love of Jesus, inspire women to be the wives and mothers God created us to be and to impact eternity—One mama at a time!

In 2016, the Help Club for Moms team completed Tommy Newberry's *40 Day Joy Challenge* and were encouraged and blessed by it. Soon emerged the idea to collaborate on developing a beautiful blend of Tommy's inspiring life coaching and Help Club's passion for pointing moms to the feet of Jesus! What ensued was *The 40 Day Joy Challenge for Moms*, a beautiful combination of Tommy's amazing videos and Help Club for Mom's inspiring writings.

Would you like to be a part of the movement?

Here's how you can get involved in the Help Club for Moms:

- *The Wise Woman Builds*, *The Wise Woman Cares*, and *The Wise Woman Enjoys* by Help Club For Moms are available on Amazon.

- Pray for the ministry and the moms in our Help Club Community worldwide--for them to know the love of Jesus and create a Christ-Like atmosphere in their homes.

- Start a Help Club for Moms group at your local church or home. We can help you!

- We are always on the lookout for Titus 2 women who can help mentor our moms through social media and prayer.

- If you are an author, blogger, graphics artist, or social media guru, we need you and your talents at the Help Club!

- We are a 501(c)(3) and all volunteer ministry! Please go to www.HelpClubForMoms.com to help us get God's Word into the hands of moms worldwide!

You can find out more about Help Club for Moms at www.HelpClubForMoms.com and on Facebook and Instagram @HelpClubForMoms.

71817941R00055

Made in the USA
Lexington, KY
24 November 2017